Broke and Alone

A Woman's Guide for Introspective Living

Da-Nel Euwings

ISBN: 9-781257-03935-7

Dedications

I dedicate this book to my wonderful son, Andre. Eleven years ago, I gave birth to the most beautiful and life-enhancing gift I've ever been given. Since then, each day of my life has been a renewed desired to be an ever greater woman, and an example of character-building qualities to you. I love you son with my whole heart and I thank you for all that you teach me little man!

I dedicate this book to my terrific brother, David. Literally, since diaper-days, you have have had my back with your example of strength, wisdom, generosity, courage, and honesty. You are a beautiful man and I thank God for you. I love you!

I dedicate this book to my beloved grandmother, affectionately nicknamed “Dutchess”. Although you are not here in the flesh, you are with me everyday in spirit. Everything I do is because of your loving example throughout my life. I pray that the woman I've become has done you proud. “Funnyface” will always remember the lessons you taught. I love you and miss you dearly.

I dedicate this book to my friend, Della. Having a real friend in this lifetime is a true blessing. Thank you for riding with me through the joys and challenges, successes and frustrations in pursuit of my dreams. I love you!

I dedicate this book to everyone who has offered their genuine and constant support to me by way of advice, coaching, encouragement, prayer, criticism, hugs, high-fives, and fist bumps. Often, your supportive words and actions arrived "right on time", when it was most needed. I appreciate your belief in me and being in the corner of a woman who had the audacity to have a dream and pursue it! I pray to continue to be a blessing to you as you have been to me. Thank you very much!

Thank you to Cheryl A. Pullins, Enrique Pascal, Angela Bolden-Thompson, and A.D. Roberts for your endorsements. As long-respected industry leaders, speakers, authors and coaches, your honest and professional feedback has been a joyful highlight for me on this project. I'm deeply grateful and honored to have your support. Thank you!

Forward

I wrote this book with a very simple motive – to help you to be the best woman you can and deserve to be. This book is not written to lecture, preach, stigmatize, generalize, berate, humiliate, or pontificate about any specific religious, political, or psychological schools of thought.

The crux of this book is not intended to teach you how to be the next billionaire nor the latest "it" woman. In principle, this book was written to help you to address, and further prevent, many attitudes and behaviors that contribute to some women living lives that hurt their themselves, their reputation, others, and wastes their resources - particularly their energy, money, and time. This book was written as if I am sitting right there with you - as a sister, friend, mother, aunt, cousin – speaking from my heart, from personal experience, and from observation, with compassion, frankness, humor, and honesty. This book was written by a right-brained thinker so I often express things in terms of metaphors or analogies.

I'm thankful for the lessons I've learned along my journey. Some lessons were like raw sandpaper and other lessons were like satin cloths that molded and polished me into the woman I love today. I have no regrets – after all, regrets are mistakes one never learned from.

Being introspective (self-examination) means that you no longer blame others, make excuses, pacify yourself, deceive yourself, procrastinate or resign yourself to a life of repetitious, senseless, preventable pains. Life is is not perfect but let me tell you, it can be a happy and fulfilling one if you choose it by focusing on the person that matters most – YOU! Enjoy your journey of growth and introspection! Brace yourself – you're about to become an even greater woman that you already are, and I applaud you!

Broke and Alone

1. Know Yourself
2. Respect Yourself
3. Educate Yourself
4. Challenge Yourself
5. Be Yourself
6. Defend Yourself
7. Trust Yourself
8. Beautify Yourself
9. Give of Yourself
10. Discipline Yourself
11. Reward Yourself
12. Love Yourself

Know Yourself

"We run away all the time to avoid coming face to face with ourselves". - Unknown

Have you ever encountered a woman that was indecisive, hesitant, anxious, unfocused, or inauthentic? There's a few reasons for this: First, the root is often because they do not have a firm grasp of who they are, or why. They usually rely of external elements to give validation and definition to who they are. Some of these sources (such as job, public figures, fans, organizations, church, possessions) are broad, fallible, and they are subjective. Another chapter (Be Yourself) will elaborate more on this unfortunate and unhealthy state of living defined by external things.

Second, such women don't have the courage or desire to look within themselves to see their naked core, seeing beyond their mask, costume, layers and defenses. I write this particular chapter from personal experience because this was me. The truth hurts, not so much when go searching for it but when we try to run away from it. For decades, I did not know who I was and whenever I dared to reveal a bit of myself, I recoiled and resorted to what was comfortable for me, or what was 'normal' to others, or what didn't cause people to judge or laugh at me (I later discovered this was a false and crippling perception and not reality). For decades, I lived a ghost life that left me exhausted, and confused. For decades, I was afraid to be noticed or heard which left me resentful and consumed. For decades, I was hungry for possibilities but was distracted and pacified by junk. For decades, I knew I was special and unique but wasn't comfortable with shining or 'bringing attention to myself'. For decades, I knew that was capable of leaving a meaningful mark but my self-identity was in question. For decades I felt like I was squeezing myself into a corset 4 sizes too small – unable to breathe comfortably or see clearly beyond mental dizziness. Why? For many reasons: I was afraid to be myself for the sake of fitting into an organization, club, clique or community. I worried about disappointing people I thought would disapprove of me. I convinced myself that there were better 'versions' of me in the world. I stressed myself out trying to march to the beat of others drums. I weakly hid behind others who were more bold, courageous, or daring. Do you see the state of mind and lifestyle this creates? Afraid. Worried. Stressed. Stunted. Artificial. Silent. Repressed. Splintered. Agitated. Disillusioned.

Listen. It takes courage to look at yourself as your really are. This is essential in order to grow and thrive financially, mentally, physically, spiritually – and thus have better relationships, finances, and prospects. I'm not talking about looking at yourself when you're glammed up and looking fly. Look at yourself on your best and worst days – beyond the compliments from admirers and flatterers. When you look at yourself, you'll see things that you absolutely love and appreciate about yourself – your skin, your voice, your creativity, your talents, your legs, your moxy, your academic intelligence, your hair, etc. But look deeper. Look at your heart. Look into the things that you don't dare speak out loud, or write in your diary or even utter in prayer. Look at the basis for the things you say, feel, think and do. The bible says that the 'heart is the origin of our motivation and our intentions'. Look at the beautiful and ugly. Look at the pleasurable as well as the painful. Look at the noble as well as the shameful. Look at the rational as well as the irrational. Look at the strengths as well as the weaknesses. Look at the openness and as well as the prejudices.

As women, we are very good at putting up appearances – to a fault. We are chameleons, able to transform ourselves into any imaginable role or personality needed to accomplish everything including 'leaping over tall buildings in a single bound'. But every superhero has a weakness. In the superhero comics, it was imperative that they knew their strengths and their weakness in order to accomplish the most good. This meant they had to acknowledge that they could at times be the conqueror as well as the defeated. When you start "feeling yourself" because of a milestone, accomplishment, compliment or improvement, it's all to easy for you to lose yourself in your ego. Another Chapter (Satisfy Yourself) will discuss the need for humble balance. Humility serves many purposes including when celebrating and rejoicing over your joys and victories however, to prevent alienating yourself or being an overly indulgent person. Being introspective about where your gifts and talents are leading you is imperative.

Doesn't it make sense the connection between spending habits and lasting relationships is the lack of knowing yourself and what is driving you? Doesn't it make sense that when your internal compass is broken or even missing you will be led anywhere by anyone? Doesn't it make sense that an empty and unidentified vessel is bound to be filled up with anything allowed to be poured into it? This is what happens when women do not know themselves, their value, or purpose. It never, ever pays to be a second-rate version of someone else rather than a first-rate version of yourself. It never, ever pays to allow others to give you your identity with their own stamp or label. After all, your label of identity to the world is your statement of worth and uniqueness that you define (and accentuate) yourself.

Remember also that knowing yourself doesn't mean to take a self inventory and then walk away from the results. Rather, this means that you are in constant and intentional growth mode – even if the growing you are doing is painful to you at times or is perplexing to others at times.

When you are introspective, it's like a constant maintenance of a home (your being); You will regularly visit your “rooms” (your heart, soul, womb, spirit, conscience, voice, attitude) which need maintenance, décor updating, and can easily accumulate unhealthy dust, bacteria, or (in one case I know of, literally) have an unknown occupant. The condition of these “rooms” affect your internal peace, comfort, balance, outlook, conversation and health. Many only take care of their “rooms” during 'Spring cleaning', New Year's, or when 'company comes', or when they're faced with a debilitating and mysterious illness. Often, it's much more costly and laborious to perform infrequent 'inventory' and 'clean out' than doing so regularly, isn't it?

Of course, we all have our favorite “room” in our home that gets the most attention and compliments – such as our intellect, swag, sex appeal, knowledge, or persona. Yet, often, women are forced to shut down because of the length of time now required to tackle the large task of self inventory, recovery, and repair of their less-visited “rooms”, due to distraction or neglect. This means expense, time away from from work, family, pleasures, and projects. Large tasks are best handled when broken down into smaller, frequent, purposeful tasks, aren't they?

Let's go further on this. What do you usually need when you're “cleaning house”? You need a trash can, disinfectant, ventilation, supporters/ professionals (when needed), rhythm, vision, and focus. Your trash can is to permanently rid yourself of the unnecessary, damaged junk that is simply taking up space within you. Your disinfectant is to thoroughly cleanse yourself of offensive, toxic, or defiling things that can spread within yourself and to others. Your ventilation is when you are open-minded and receptive to fresh and cleansing 'air' from healthy and positive sources. Your rhythm is your own musical tempo and pace – not in comparison to anyone else. Your vision is your desired outcome that will bring you joy and satisfaction. Your focus is what will keep you persistent, disciplined, and undeterred on your journey. As I stated, don't be afraid or ashamed to have a trusted, mature, experienced (even a professional) adviser to help you to be accountable for the regular cleaning and beautifying of your "rooms". The caution is to not delegate matters that are truly your responsibility to personally address meditatively/prayerfully. Ultimately, you have to live in your "home" and live with the condition it is in. Finally, knowing yourself means also knowing why you are unable to move forward on some things and what your influencers are. Link about it: Weights are used for two reasons - to keep you grounded (as protection) or to hinder your growth (as restriction). Learn the differences between the two, and identify WHO or WHAT are the weight in your life, and how they are protecting or restricting you from being your best self. Be honest – even if it is yourself or someone close to you – and accept, adjust, remove the weights accordingly.

Understand: Getting to know yourself takes time, courage and effort. It isn't easy and can be very telling, but you can do it. Once you truly know yourself then your choices, reactions, moods, needs, cravings, and impulses won't catch you unawares (as if you are a stranger in your own body) but you will know what is in your best interests and won't be afraid of, or unfamiliar with yourself.

Think: Would you sell a product or service to someone if you aren't even familiar with it yourself? Why would that person want to buy something of undefined use or value? Couldn't that person hold you accountable for selling something that is false, unhealthy, or even dangerous? Wouldn't you be more convincing and require a less-forced sales pitch? Do you get it? When you are “selling” yourself to the world (meaning: presenting yourself as you know yourself to be) you can be the best thing that ever happened to someone or the worst, all because of what you do or don't know about yourself. Related to this analogy: When you know yourself – your value and potential – you will never, ever allow anyone to put a clearance sign on you, limiting the happiness and prosperity that you DESERVE!

HOW CAN KNOWING YOURSELF PREVENT YOU FROM BEING BROKE AND ALONE?

____

____

____

____

____

____

____

____

____

____

____

____

____

____

Respect Yourself

"If you put a really small value upon yourself, rest assured that the world will not raise your price." - Unknown

This chapter addresses a topic that was the basis for major changes I made in my life once I "got it": respect for yourself is revealed in everything you say and do, respect for yourself is not dependent on your mood, possessions, or other externals, and respect for yourself should never be delegated to anyone else. One definition of respect is "to show honor, esteem, appreciation, admiration, or consideration". Although I cared about how I carried myself (raised in pretty strict home), it's not the same as self respect which takes time to cultivate, appreciate, and was evident by how I allow myself to be treated. This was also true in relationships (romantic, personal, and professional), habits, conversations, and outlook. Interestingly, the disrespect I opened myself to and tolerated from others was not always blatant but was instead subtle overtime. At times, I settled in situations that betrayed respect for myself - a job position, relationship, or friendship - deceiving myself with the unhealthy reasoning that I would simply endure, be silent, adapt, cry privately, make excuses, or toughen up. Respect for yourself is something you must believe is yours to have and certainly not resorting to stealing it or buying it.

In Madonna's song, “Respect Yourself”, one line goes, “Don't go for second best baby. Put your love to the test. You deserve the best in life...so if the time isn't right then move on.” There's many takeaways from this – for romantic, personal and business matters. If you've set your standards low and you're willing to accept second best then that's what you'll likely get. If you hastily reach for the apples on the ground – which are likely rotten and worthless - rather than making patient intelligent effort to grab a 'top apple', then you're cheating yourself of healthy, beautiful, satisfying fruit. This principle is true in all aspects of your life.

Like it or not, in order for you to obtain the best in life then you must demonstrate that you ARE the best recipient for it. Like it or not, people value their time and reputation more than they value yours – and will deal with you accordingly. Like it or not, people will make fast judgments based on limited interactions – even if it is your 'off' day. Like it or not, bad news or negative gossip spreads faster than good news. Like it or not, people are less tolerant of greedy people who take things they haven't earned. Like it or not, there are no guarantees you'll be given a second chance to recover from a social or professional faux pas. Like it or not, people will often treat you based on how you treat yourself.

Many women constantly shout and stamp their feet to their children, to their boss, to their mates, to their friends loudly demanding that they be respected. Why would you need to stamp and shout to receive something from those who know the REAL you? If they know your value, wouldn't they accord it to you? If they don't now the real you, has your value been diluted, covered, or diminished in some way?

Consider: Are your words unnecessarily and constantly vulgar? Do you befriend others who detract from or even defile your good name. Do you prostitute yourself for the spotlight? Are you having unprotected sex and/or having sex with someone you know you should not be with? Does your clothing scream “desperate slut”? Does your drinking or other 'vices' cause more embarrassment than relaxation for you and those in your company? Does your attitude repel people? Do you live in denial about your unhealthy weight? Do you invest more money on your nails, weaves, parties, or shoes then in nurturing your mate, children, home/car maintenance, education, retirement savings, or business? Do you callously say, “I'm doing me” without considering the setting, your future, or your relationships?

How can you possibly ask others to respect you – professionally, romantically, or otherwise – if you don't give them reasons to? Why should a quality employer give a quality job to a less-than qualified applicant? Why should your children do as you say when they don't respect what you do? Why should a quality romantic partner and prospective mate maintain a quality relationship with a less-than qualified woman? Why should a respectable friend, business collaborator, client or benefactor align themselves with a less-than-qualified person? Why should you be puzzled about having unhealthy hair, skin, weight, emotions, when you aren't treating your body like something precious and desirable? Why should your home be a haven of cleanliness and peace when your words, habits or invited guests don't show respect? Why should burned bridges be repaired if you don't acknowledge your role in its demise in the first place?

Like it or not, respect for yourself, therefore is not something that you scream for, buy or demand. Respect is commanded (definition: to deserve and receive as due) and is earned. Respect can be lost. Respect denotes honor, dignity and value which is more than being a person who is merely tolerated by others. Check your self-respect gauge daily to make sure you aren't ever on “Empty”. Be sure to fuel yourself with complementary, elevated and uplifting thoughts – which precedes complimentary actions - to always remain “Full” of respect for yourself rather than just full of yourself. It can be done and it's so worth your effort!

HOW CAN RESPECTING YOURSELF PREVENT YOU FROM BEING BROKE AND ALONE?

____

Educate Yourself

"Education is the key to unlock the golden door of freedom." - George Washington Carver

For me, education was at times a chore because I always knew that I was an intelligent person but yet I always saw things from different perspectives, and had a different learning style than most formalized systems could adapt to. For instance, I'm primarily a kinesthetic, right-brain learner. (Others may be more auditory, visual, or left-brain). By understanding my learning style as artistic and abstract I was finally able to research, study, debate, engage, probe, explore, investigate, inquire, observe, weigh, verify, and question things that I believed and how they affected my choices, outlook, connections and future. I was finally able to satisfy my eager appetite for learning and make the most OF what I was learning. That's what being an educated woman means to me. There's three areas of education that I want you to consider: Academic Education, Spiritual Education, and Life Education.

On the matter of academic education: this serves the purpose for you to improve your career prospects, sharpen necessary technical skills, or provide mental stimulation. In today's market, it's almost a necessity for women to have secondary education of some sort in order to have a competitive edge since we earn far less than men. Of course, it is not a guarantee to a charmed life, nor does acquiring a degree make you better than other women – or worse off if you don't. Many of us know women who have degrees but they haven't really applied the information, or they have become “so smart that they're stupid” (an apropos quote from my deceased grandmother) as will be discussed in a moment. Have you asked yourself or a trusted adviser if your goals will be better obtained with increased academic education under your belt? Opportunities abound for online courses, community colleges, self-study programs, and many options are low cost, free, or obtained by scholarships or apprenticeships. For instance, many women don't know how to interpret a balance sheet, don't know their income tax bracket, don't know who their local Councilman is, can't name two popular stocks, how to change a faucet washer, what kind of oil to put in their car, what foods trigger common illnesses, how use their computer safely, or even read cultural material regularly.

Now, unless it is your schtick, you don't necessarily need to become an expert in finances, home repair, auto mechanics, nutrition, politics, info technology, or world history but it helps you to be conversant and aware of situations and issues that affect you, your family, your income, etc.

Understand: This doesn't mean that you endeavor simply to gain head knowledge for superficial reasons, or merely to brag or aloofly elevate yourself above others. Your endeavor instead, should be to satisfy the natural human desire to explore, stretch, and improve. Find your niche, your gift and then build upon it, stay current, competitive, aware, and then parlay what you already know into other avenues that can give more depth to your life. The point is this: Would your mind be sharper, your finances improved, your mistakes fewer, your conversations more engaging, your network of quality people enlarged, your outlook broadened, your career/professional goals elevated, your confidence heightened?

On the matter of spiritual education: it is my opinion that one's motive in acquiring more spiritual facts/ quotes/ scriptures should be greater than solely following an organized religion, or a charismatic person, or occupying an overflowing building. It is a very real fact that humans will disappoint us and buildings are a mere shell. Your spiritual connection and your divine reason for existing should not hinge on blind credulity, nor on an imperfect person or a building. When that happens, it leads to disillusionment, confusion, emptiness, bitterness, and loneliness by those who could not function using their own power of reason, judgment and good sense on their own. The danger is what we see happening all over the world today: fanaticism, prejudice, fear, hatred, and division - the very opposites of what Spirituality is supposed to encourage – unity, peace, introspection, love, compassion, and respect. One should seek and nurture their own personal unbreakable bond with your Supreme Source of life and guidance rather than following a practice out of duty, pressure, luck, fear, or coercion.

Being religious is not the same as being spiritual. There are thousands of doctrines, opinions, faiths, cults, theories, and there are Beings that are called by different Names, and regarded by many with love - and regarded by others with disdain. Therefore, I encourage you to use your inner good sense, power of reason, shrewd judgment, self awareness, and rational thought processes to ask the following of yourself when considering your spiritual education: Are you seeking meaning in your life? Are you grieving, angry, hurt, disillusioned? Is your partner, spouse, or close person-of-influence suggesting you adopt their spiritual practices? How will your practice affect your current or future household? What comparative research have you done? What are your own motives? Is this a curiosity or an intellectual phase for you? Do you have a chemical imbalance that can be exacerbated or abused? How much of your time, money and energy are you willing to commit in your pursuit? What will you gain? What will you be sacrificing? These are necessary questions to ask aren't they?

On the matter of life education: "It is hard to fill a cup which is already full." (from the movie, "Avatar") LESSON: There's always some way you can improve yourself but only if you are humble, pliable, introspective, honest, and ready to clean out any 'junk' filling up your cup. No matter how many years you have lived, situations you have experienced, problems you have endured, tragedies you've observed, there is always something life can further teach the humble, honest and hungry. Many live life with their heads down, or with their faces stuck in a mirror. Living with your head down out of denial, fear, embarrassment, boredom or disillusionment means that many valuable lessons and experiences are passing you by. Living your life with your face stuck in a mirror, that is, living a life fueled by egotism, selfishness, vanity, arrogance, and disinterest in others means that many interpersonal skills and character-building lessons will be absent from your well of wisdom. As I mentioned previously, my beloved deceased grandmother, "Dutchess", used to say 'some people are so smart they're stupid'. What I now understand from her statement is that the acquisition of knowledge will do no good if it isn't absorbed into the mind, heart and spirit of a person, it is fully understood, digested, appreciated, lived and shared. We call this common sense, which we all know is not so common. Educating yourself means that you don't instantly react to every new trend, the hottest hype, the loudest peacock (those who constantly fan their feathers for your attention), or bounce on the new shiny bandwagon. By the way, regarding the term, "bandwagon", think about it: Isn't a wagon meant to be pulled by the thing it's attached to? Are you carefully doing your due diligence, ensuring that the "band" that you're attached to and being pulled by is really for you? Many are in business – and get paid extremely well – to manipulate, sell, bait-and-trap people.

When we are ignorant, uninformed, naïve, desperate, bored, isolated, emotionally damaged or lazy, it's all too easy to become the target and prey of such types who will soak us – like a dry sponge – with theories, opinions, dogmas, mantras, pitches and slogans that may be completely misaligned with our purpose. Change can be a great thing, but make sure that your changes are "life enhancers" rather than "life complicators". Then, remember to be generous and share what you learn to those who are in need of valuable and timely gems as well. Your life is enriched and gratifying when you don't idly watch others stumble and fall and look down on them but instead impart your wisdom gained out of empathy (just as you have liked been a recipient as well). An educated woman is an empowered woman.

HOW CAN EDUCATING YOURSELF PREVENT YOU FROM

BEING BROKE & ALONE?

____

____

____

____

____

____

____

____

____

____

____

____

____

____

Challenge Yourself

"You have powers you never dreamed of. You can do things you never thought you could do. There are no limitations in what you can do except in the limitations of your own mind."

D. P. Kingsley

Complacency. Laziness. Disillusionment. Fear. Doubt. Weariness. Distrust. Isolation. Weakness. Confusion. These are some of the reasons why a woman's development becomes repressed, stunted and unrealized. All living beings should be in a constant state of renewal, development, improvement, and growth. You'll often find yourself alone or withdrawn when you aren't feeling stimulated, inspired or intrigued with the wonders of life. If you aren't pushing yourself, tapping into your fullest potential, then you're not really living your fullest life possible. If you're constantly taking the path of least resistance, not taking any risks, not "daydreaming" of possibilities, not exploring your curiosities, not stretching your muscles to get out of your comfort zone and safety corner, just "sliding by" under the radar (at work, at school, in your groups) then you are not really living. If you find yourself repeating your same old quotes, data, facts, or jokes, year after year in conversation (especially if it wasn't the proper audience or timing) then you're beginning to lack depth and substance mentally and spiritually. Isn't your mind your most valuable muscle (aside from your heart) and doesn't it require constant strengthening and nourishment? What you feed it – or don't feed it – will be very evident in your actions, attitude and behaviors, contributing to a life that is rich and stimulating or a life that is mundane, fruitless and wasteful. If it doesn't bring you joy don't empower it (Selectivity). If it doesn't amplify your morals don't embrace it (Dignity). If it can't be fixed today don't exacerbate it (Prudence). If you can't make up your mind don't rush into it (Forethought). That is my formula for being a truly well-rounded woman.

Of course you need to understand: No one can be a superstar in everything they pursue. No one is an expert at everything they do. No one succeeds at everything they explore. No one reaps an overflowing bounty from every seed they plant. No one gets an "A" in every class they've ever taken. No one walks on a perfectly paved path to success. No one has a real-life "Midas Touch".

To illustrate how mental cages limits your options and achievements, think about the difference between dolphins (my favorite mammal) living in the wild ocean versus the ones living in captivity. Among some disadvantages of captivity, they have shorter life spans, less maneuverability, less food variety, and less natural-peer stimulation. In contrast, while they are in the wild, majority of their time is spent in deep exploration, natural play, endless varieties of food, mate selection, and mental stimulation.

Do you get it? When you make yourself a captive of your own mind, by choosing to limit your reading repertoire, social interaction, creative opportunities, professional input, or peer circle to only those that simply reflect your current (and possibly grossly outdated or incorrect) viewpoints and creatively sterile lifestyle, then you are like that dolphin in captivity – surviving but not really thriving. Alive but not really living.

Related to this the need for maturity, patience, and foresightedness. How many times have you prayed or begged for the immediate end to a problem you were dealing with? Often, many will pay very dearly (financially, reputation, emotionally) when seeking a quick exit or instant fix instead of using creative thinking and critical thinking to skillfully work through it. If you are a parent/guardian perhaps you've explained this concept to a child – courage pays off when you stand up to challenges that seem to be like mountainous bullies.

When you confront fear and walk up to it, it really looks smaller. Obviously, this is easier said then done, especially if you are already in 'recovery mode' from a recent difficulty, or if this challenge is completely new, if it hits a sensitive spot, or if you're already in the middle of an existing difficulty. Yet, when you encounter a huge challenge, isn't the victory sweeter when you surpass your own expectations – and even those of negative naysayers? Isn't the triumph exhilarating after your mind, heart, vision, imagination and resolve have been stretched, lengthened and strengthened?

Despair, defeatism, negativity, complaining, blaming, & anxiety doesn't solve problems. Focused action, persistence with purpose, individualized creativity, genuine humility, selective open mindedness, and keen foresightedness does. "Get busy living or get busy dying" (my favorite quote from movie, "The Shawshank Redemption"). Also remember that when you unapologetically insist on QUALITY versus QUANTITY you have more room in your mind, heart, home, and life for what matters most. Taking shortcuts or the path of least resistance often yields fruit that is fast but unripened, bitter, temporary, or worthless. When you take shortcuts and not challenge yourself – as with other paths, such as a marathon race, or a road trip – you can often injure yourself, get lost and waste time and resources just to back-peddle to do the task right from the beginning. Challenging yourself however, includes examining yourself to see how you can bend, flex, stretch, push, and evolve so that you will thrive. Therefore, I encourage you to not take shortcuts in life and in your relationships but instead nurture them, watch them, dote over them, protect them, value them, respect them, adjust with them, and invest in them. Finally, LIFE IS A BUFFET! Get your own plate - don't steal others' food and don't be a "hog" - greed is so unattractive. Embrace variety. Diversity is healthy for you. Explore and see what you've been missing.

HOW CAN CHALLENGING YOURSELF PREVENT YOU FROM

BEING BROKE AND ALONE?

____

____

____

____

____

____

____

____

____

____

____

____

____

____

Be Yourself

“The most exhausting thing in life is being insincere.” - Anne Morrow Lindbergh

The moment I try to imitate someone, it rarely works well for me. It rarely feels authentic or “me”. It rarely feels like my skin but instead feels like a costume. And those who know the real me can often see right through that thin carbon copy.

Understand: There's a distinct difference between “imitation” and “duplication”. The difference is the intent. By definition, imitation means to copy, or to follow as a model. When you notice the correct way to wear a sari, match makeup to your skin tone, save money on groceries, the best summer camp, get a smart investment tip, or a gas friendly automobile and , these don't necessarily define your own knowledge, existence or identity and hence this is imitation – essentially harmless. When, however, you base every choice, thought, action on everything that another person does because you lack your own purpose and drive, want to compete, impress, need validation, approval, applause, attention and you essentially want to BE that person then you are merely a duplication – a copy – with so many possible harmful affects to you and others affected by your disingenuous 'life'.

Think: What happens when you photocopy an original document of something? Aren't the subsequent photocopies more faded, more blurred, and more distorted than the original? Don't you often have to struggle to 'read' the photocopy for clear meaning? How about when you make a photocopy a photocopy OF a photocopy? Do you get the point? Everyone prefers to deal with originals.

Because of the proliferation of painful and costly scandals, people today have less and less tolerance for being misled or bamboozled by those who misrepresent themselves or their abilities, those who cheat their way into 'inner circles', those who pass off stolen ideas as their own, those who don't practice what they preach, those who have no depth to their opinions, or those who ride the skirt tails of others' hard earned success.

A movie that comes to mind is “Single White Female”. When I first saw this movie, it totally freaked me out. The character “Hedy” did many unimaginable things to copy and acquire her roommate's ("Allie") life that she desperately wanted to live – her hair, clothes, speech, movements, even sleeping with Allie's boyfriend (yep, sick!). Now, of course this movie is a very extreme version of what an emotionally damaged person did, however the undeniable point still is this: Be careful about living a false life. Be yourself.

It's important to realize also that someone always knows the real you. The world has gotten smaller making formerly exclusive or hidden circles more transparent, making formerly aloof or reclusive people more accessible, making formerly distant connections more personal. It is true that we all need to occasionally adapt and adjust our clothing, speech, or mannerisms to fit a setting, career or occasion – there's a time and place for everything. Yet, if our core self is so diluted to where we are totally unrecognizable or even appearing , forced, phoney and disingenuous then we have to pause and ask what our purpose is and it's subsequent cost. Many women have indeed found themselves alone because being a turnoff to others and coming off as as a robotic charlatan. Also consider:

When you “borrow” things from others – someone's dreams, someone's swag, someone's man, someone's friends - don't you realize that your life own lacks depth because nothing you say, think or do is your own? A real life takes real work!

If you don't like yourself as you currently are, then consider counseling to explore the reasons why you don't, to identify what makes you unique and valuable, then to accentuate the positive!

HOW CAN BEING YOURSELF PREVENT YOU FROM BEING

BROKE AND ALONE?

____

____

____

____

____

____

____

____

____

____

____

____

____

____

Protect Yourself

"Self preservation is the first law of nature". - Unknown

Some would argue that this quote contributes to selfishness, defensiveness, close-mindedness, vanity, mistrust, neurotic or egocentric behavior. That's not what I'm suggesting you become. If these are your predominant traits then you will indeed find yourself broke and alone because you've chosen to build more walls than bridges.

Because of insecurity and fear, I built walls to keep out people that I should have let it and mistakenly let people in who did not deserve a place in my life. Of course, no one has a crystal ball and can foresee how relationships will unfold however extremes are never good, on either side of the spectrum – being too trusting and being generally mistrustful without cause. As with all principles, balance is the key. What I want you to consider is learn to better protect yourself mentally, financially, and physically. For instance: How do you react when someone upsets you? If you're easily prone to fly off the handle at every annoyance, then your protective skin is very thin and you'll constantly be in repair mode. What do you do when you receive a large sum of money (job bonus, lawsuit settlement, tax refund, loan reimbursement, lottery winnings)? If your first act is to go splurge and party before addressing your obligations then your financial protection will remain weak. How do you react when you have a craving for a jumbo cheese steak with everything on it, or steamy sex with someone new, or a new pair of Christian Louboutins on your near-maxed out credit card, or the desire to tell off someone who upset you? If you're primarily an impulsive and compulsive person acting recklessly and thoughtlessly on every urge then your financial, physical, professional, and emotional wellness will surely be in jeopardy. Doesn't this make sense?

Also, on this matter of protecting yourself: On one hand, many have lost their ideas, money, reputation, spirit, health, and dreams because of being too lax in judgment, being too trusting without reason, being too familiar without caution, being too risky without common sense, being too free-spirited without any moral boundaries. If you haven't noticed, I love alliteration: Due diligence, discretion, and discernment are so important in this area. So are shrewdness, sensibility, self-control and sensitivity. Furthermore, don't squander your time, heart, money or reputation nor allow anyone to wrangle these from you. Waste & recklessness have high price tags - potentially leaving you physically, emotionally, financially & spiritually bankrupt.

Consider: How many times have we encountered people who we felt were put into our lives 'for a reason'. Do you often understand the reason? Many are in your life to either drain you or to train you! Many are true leeches and abusers who are all about their own agenda and needs – often shamelessly, brazenly, illegally, and unapologetically. All of us at some point are opportunists – taking advantage of an opportunity that can meet our own agenda and needs. Your task is to first know what you are being asked to give, at what cost, to whom, and why BEFORE you make your mind, heart, money, body, or life accessible to anyone. Not all who want something from you should be immediately dismissed but should be dealt with in limited doses to protect yourself, because you can gain valuable training that will serve you well.

Consider this training: When a boxer steps into a ring, she needs to become skilled at both offensive and defensive stances. When she is in the offensive, that is when she is most vulnerable – her jaw/head/torso are exposed, her stance is off level, her focus is shifted but, that is when she learns the most. She learns from the blows. You may not like it, but being in “learning mode” does help protect you, teach you, toughen you, embolden you, and strengthen you. You may not like it when others deliver the blows (regardless of their intentions) but they are all lessons if you control your emotions, and remember why you are in the ring in the first place.

Another protective measure is to remember not to expect things from people who do not have a vested interest in you. What does this mean? One dictionary defines “vested interest” as: “having personal stake, or expectation of personal gain that underlies a strong commitment to maintain or influence an action”. Break this down: How loyal can a person really be to you who only has a passing interest in you? Many are easily distracted by the next new shiny thing that catches their eye. Unless people have made a financial, legal, or emotional attachment to you, often there is no reason whatsoever to expect their solid or reliable allegiance. This is one trap that befalls many women who mistake compliments, flattery, favors or accolades as signs to cling to, marry, or support those who do not reciprocate what was given to them. By nature, people are loyal to something once they see they have a measure of control or influence over it – as was stated in the above definition. Therefore, another element of protecting yourself is understanding who you give your control to, and who you allow to influence you.

Moving forward on this topic: The other side of the coin is realizing that some of the greatest ideas and relationships are forged when one person "takes a leap of faith"or "takes a chance" on an unique opportunity. Before you start leaping into big things however, why not train your intuition, your common sense, your read on people, your personal needs, your awareness of social/ economic trends on smaller everyday things. Think: Why try to bench press 200lbs when you can barely lift 90lbs? Try building up your muscle/ your personal protective strength by considering:

Is the business collaboration you're considering financially sensible? Should you be sleeping with the person you're considering sleeping with, and are you using protection? Is your confidant a reputable and mature person? Is your idea of investing in yourself a weekly drinking/ shopping/ partying spree? Do you diligently monitor your credit worthiness and savings for your future? Do you only think about maintaining healthy diet and weight during New Year's resolutions? Are the things you read, or are the people you follow infecting you with cancerous character/career-sabotaging ideas? Are you enabling the fruitless habits and drama-filled lives of people who aren't ready to grow up? Does your routine, clothing, conversation, spending, or vices leave you potentially exposed to abuse, extreme debt, sickness, waste, depression, of frustration? Is your time spent daydreaming about fantasies from novels or others' perceived lives? Will the situation or temptation you face matter five minutes from now, five days from now, or five years from now? (This memorable "5-5-5 rule" is courtesy of my wise brother, David.)

Also, caution is in order: Be careful about what you endorse. Before you jump on a nonspecific or vague request for prayer, cheering, money, rallying or support, make sure you understand what your name will be attached to and contributing to. This helps protects you from sharing in any blame for matters you did not fully understand – many people are not completely honest or accurate when they present their causes to us.

Going forward, consider it your obligation to regularly examine your defenses for necessity and durability - as you would for another other element (your home, immune system, your credit, etc.) - to help minimize unhealthy and damaging 'invaders' and thieves.

HOW CAN PROTECTING YOURSELF PREVENT YOU FROM

BEING BROKE AND ALONE?

____

____

____

____

____

____

____

____

____

____

____

____

____

____

Trust Yourself

"As soon as you trust yourself you will learn how to live." Joann Wolfgang von Goethe

Because I made so many mistakes, I deemed myself no longer worthy of trust. How foolish. Making mistakes is part of life. Regrets are mistakes that you simply did not learn from. Once I realized this I no longer had regrets – because I'd learned from the lessons - I became my most trusted source for direction (second only to my Creator). I can't tell you how refreshing it was (to the point of tears) when I reached that moment. Before that, I was incredibly indecisive, hesitant, nervous, and codependent on others that I began to feel stunted rather than liberated and I looked to others to pull and push me. Understand: I am not saying that you dismiss valid, verifiable, well-meaning, advice, criticism, and feedback. That would be to your detriment, counterproductive and unattractive to do so.

Your gut is the bi-product of all that you've ingested and digested. It stands to reason that if you're selective about what you take in, absorb, buy into then your gut will become a part of you, fueling your desires, fears, curiosities, and needs. Your gut (intuition) is faulty and is not a perfect gauge however it does have a purpose. (A "cousin" to this is your conscience but that pertains more to what you believe to be moral or ethical and is not the point of this topic and is a different matter.) Intuition is one of the best assets we've been given. When we opt to behave like robots – being solely dependent on other for motivation, ideas, zeal, or purpose then how fulfilling will our lives really be? One reason why many find themselves alone is because of not trusting in themselves for inspiration, not listening to their inner gut, their inner voice. Then, when the external sources of validation and existence disappoint, or leave then they are left empathy, bitter, exposed, and unfulfilled. This is why regular meditation and purposeful silence is so important. You need to silence the competing external voices, listen to your rhythm, hear what you've been ignoring, face what you've been covering up, reveal the hidden gems, embrace what's screaming for attention. You may not always like how your gut makes you feel – sometimes it will be on-point, or you may feel it is incorrect, and sometimes it will compel you to make drastic movements and adjustments that will propel you forward and soar beautifully. They key is to learn to trust that you know your own pulse, tempo, breath, itch, urge, and vision. After all, if you can't trust yourself, how can you learn to trust others? If you are prone to constant hesitancy, fear and procrastination, how can anyone develop confidence in you? If always make your decisions only after a public consensus (to solicit what you want to hear versus what you need to hear) whose life are you living? If you can not courageously take a stand for your values, principles, goals, friends, loved ones then how can you expect anyone to be in your corner? If you don't train your senses (awareness and sensitivity of the things seen and things unseen) will they be of good use to you? If you choose to primarily listen to other's voices for permission to act, think, or breathe, how will you recognize your own inner voice when it speaks?

Trusting yourself will enable you to be able to learn to trust those when there is a basis to. Being burned in the past and fear are often reasons why many can not or will not trust others. You have to realize that you isolate and stunt yourself when you deprive yourself of rewarding and lasting connections that await quality women. Be very careful not to hastily or wantonly dismiss people – especially those who may seem insignificant or 'ordinary' . Remember, the “nerds”, shy, reserved, and unassuming people are, and have become some of the most endearing, intelligent, respected and materially wealthy people on earth. What you pass over today may be cherished by someone else tomorrow. Many don't notice a squandered blessing until someone else finds & cherishes it.

Of course, trust takes time to build up so I encourage you in small ways daily to learn to awaken your self actualization, developing your fullest potential - particularly as appoint yourself your most trusted advocate, and protector of your interests.

HOW CAN TRUSTING YOURSELF PREVENT YOU FROM BEING BROKE AND ALONE?

____

____

____

____

____

____

____

____

____

____

____

____

____

____

Beautify Yourself

"Like a ring of gold in a pig's snout, so is a beautiful woman who lacks sense."

Proverbs 11:22

This scripture is so meaty and self explanatory, I could stop right here and go on the the next chapter. But let's dig into this a little. How often have you seen an sharp, attractive, intriguing, stylish woman with all kinds of swag and popularity, but then her words or behaviors were instantly a foul turnoff to you? There's no shortage of commercials, celebrity-backed makeup lines, image consultants, fashionistas in the business of ultimately getting you to spend big bucks and time focusing on the outer person – although their agenda is neatly packaged as "We care about you". The intense pressure and hype is unbelievable. I have nothing against those whose skills, education and experience help women look more polished, powerful, and professional for their career, life change, or makeover. Believe me, I get it: In today's world, you are sized up in less than 10 seconds based on your appearance alone, before you even open your mouth on a date, before you present your resume at a job fair, before you give your elevator pitch to a business prospect.

Believe me, I get it: Your first impression begins with what people can see in order for them to consider giving your the time of day. Believe me, I get it: Since people's attention is short, you need to stand out in some way and being 'beautiful', bold, and bodacious is the commonly expected way to be. But after you remove your costume – hair pieces, eyelashes, acrylic nails, makeup, stilettos, bling, and send home your fan club, would anyone still like YOU? Real beauty is NOT only skin deep. It is from within the inner depths of your heart, mind, and spirit and radiates outwardly. Therefore it stands to reason that if you are ugly on the inside (damaged, bitter, arrogant, greedy, amoral, vulgar or hostile) then it will find its way to the surface, evident in your speech and actions no matter how magazine-cover-ready you look.

Are your conversations mostly about non- substantive matters? Are you self absorbed? Have you spent an exorbitant amount of money and time on cosmetics, clothing and a lifestyle yet you are still emotionally unhealthy? Do you manipulate conversations and people without regard? Are you a "spotlight prostitute" – shameless stomping into the limelight even at inappropriate times?

Many women go through great pains and expense to maintain the exterior - waxing, laser, braids, microsurgery, chemical peels, weaves, tattoo makeup, & hotdog-tight corsets, to name a few. But like most alterations to our exterior, it is often indicative of how we feel on the inside. Of course, many women have opted for corrective procedures because of health or personal reasons. There's nothing wrong with that - it's your body, and it's a magnificent canvas ready for you to express your individuality, beliefs, milestones, etc. My caution to you is to never alter your body to primarily please anyone else but yourself, count the cost (present & future), and be real about your motives and desired outcome. If you are emotionally damaged, in turmoil, reckless, insecure, empty, or obsessive it will be apparent in how you define beauty. When people say, "beauty is in the eye of the beholder", the primary person who should approve of your beauty is you - as long as the mirror you're looking in is not distorted by devaluing, detracting, or dehumanizing ideas or standards that will not enhance your inner beauty at all. The great thing about being a woman is that we have many shades and moods - sultry, reserved, sassy, shy, sexy, funky, classic, or eclectic. Just don't be a phoney or a hypocrite.

The key is to remember that what you do to your exterior should be like adding gems to a crown, not onto a pig (as stated in the opening

Proverb). Looking fly but acting foul, looking hot but acting cold, looking flawless but harping on other's flaws, looking runway-ready but behaving like a runaway fool, looking clean and shiny but always scratching to outshine, looking like you robbed a bank but having no money in a bank, looking like your life is golden but you're personality is dark will surely alienate yourself and even embarrass yourself eventually.

Real beauty never fades, it is never forced, it comes from within, it is constantly enhanced, it seamlessly carries over in all settings, and is unique to you – like a snowflake, no two are the same!

HOW DOES BEUTIFYING YOURSELF PREVENT YOU FROM

BEING BROKE AND ALONE?

____

____

____

____

____

____

____

____

____

____

____

____

____

____

Give of Yourself

"To be rich in admiration and free from envy, to rejoice greatly in the good of others, to love with such generosity of heart that your love is still a dear possession in absence of unkindness – these are the gifts which money cannot buy."

Robert Louis Stevenson

I've learned that when I bless others, I am in turn blessed by others. When I do, I don't blow a trumpet, nor do I solicit public props. That's not my style. If the recipients choose to publicly express gratitude for something I've done from my heart, I'm graciously appreciative. Remember: People will be turned off by what I call "spotlight prostitutes" so, check your motives.

In my opinion and from observation, when you are self-absorbed, living a life that's all about you to the exclusion of other's needs and feelings, you're really living a lack-luster, one-dimensional life. If you have acquired material, professional, academic, spiritual, and financial experience and yet you selfishly keep it all to yourself then what is the point? Haven't you yourself been the direct or indirect recipient of what others have gained?

Of course, when deciding to be hospitable, philanthropic, and generous, you need to be very clear on several things: What individuals, entities, causes, or organizations do you want to support, why, and how? Will you be specific in clearly establishing any mutual expectations? How will any alignments or collaborations impact your reputation, finances, time, relationships, and mission?

Understand: The trap that befalls many women is the mistaken idea that they must be all things to all people. This is unrealistic and foolish. Our ego can convince us that we are invincible: be everywhere, do everything, be all things, be all knowing, be superheros, be superstars. This is unreasonable, unhealthy and unbalanced, and leads to increased debt, misappropriated energies, misunderstandings, health issues, relationship strain, career anxieties, and resentment. It takes patient forethought and selectivity to know where and how your gifts will be best needed and valued.

There are many that you will encounter who will add and multiply your life's happiness however there are those that will simply subtract and divide from it. It's up to you to learn the difference so that when you selflessly give of yourself it will not be in vain or with constant imbalance, or lack of acknowledgment or appreciation. Giving of yourself in your personal and professional relationships may not always be reciprocated or regularly noticed but your character still becomes refined and strengthened when you give of yourself. We live in a world of takers, moochers, cheaters, opportunists and leeches. This sometimes unfortunately causes good people to recoil and refrain from allowing their gifts, knowledge and resources to be seen, celebrated, and appreciated. But believe me, it's refreshing to be around a woman who observes the needs of others and is courteous and generous, not as a front nor for show but out of sincerity. In fact, it's really unbecoming to look down on others unless you're helping them up. Also, don't always wait for others to make the first move of kindness but instead be the beacon - be the exemplar. Selfless and kind acts definitely has a self-healing effect, a ripple effect, as well as a boomerang effect. First, when were are enduring our own problems, it is often best for us to volunteer, mentor or offer tangible support to others in need to prevent us being self-consumed while our difficulties are worked out. Second, you just never know the far-reaching affects your actions may have on others or yourself. Finally, when you 'sow bountifully you reap bountifully'. You may not be on the cover of a magazine or on a TV show for your deeds however if you train your senses, you may realize that you have often received blessings, favors, gifts or assistance that you may not have expected. One of my favorite movies, “Pay It Forward” is based on premise that one selfless and purposeful act (some call, “random acts of kindness”) does indeed help change the dynamics and health of the world. Doing so regularly and wholeheartedly is very endearing, refreshing and attractive to others.

HOW DOES GIVING OF YOURSELF PREVENT YOU FROM

BEING BROKE AND ALONE?

Discipline Yourself

"Self-disciplined begins with the mastery of your thoughts. If you don't control what you think, you can't control what you do. Simply, self-discipline enables you to think first and act afterward." - Napoleon Hill

We live in a world of instant gratification – get who or what you can as fast and effortlessly as possible, regardless of the cost or pain incurred by us or someone else. Getting what you can and deeply enjoying what you get are not the same thing. Wanting something and needing something are not the same thing. Deserving something and earning something are not the same thing. This is why honestly, clearly and regularly identifying your needs versus your wants is so important. Self control, restraint, patience, and contentment are not words that we like to hear – especially if we grew up in a dictatorial home or school that left a harsh taste in our mouths, or if we lived in poverty and thus convince ourselves that excessively indulgent living makes up for what we may have lacked in childhood.

We often resort being like the two-year old who doesn't like to hear the word, “no”. We then pout, whine, get an attitude, abandon our current joys, and jealously covet what others have with an insatiable desire that we will do almost anything to get what we feel is ours to have. We will even vehemently convince ourselves – and rally others who will pray, and cheer for us – that our lives will simply end unless we've obtained our newest craving or interest. Envy is unattractive and is dangerous to your mental and physical health. The funny thing is, often, that thing you desire that belongs to others may be something you can't handle or maintain even if you did receive it. Be careful of what you envy and what you wish for, especially when you're looking at others from a limited view.

Marketers, sales people, and advertisers often do not care if you really don't have the budget, skills, or mental acumen to acquire the things that they make seem available to you. How many times have you heard that “anything worth having is worth waiting for, working for, and fighting for?' Isn't it true that when you get something very easily and quickly (e.g. job, sex, money, possessions, weight loss) that it just isn't quite as satisfying as when you struggled, worked, sacrificed, hungered, and persevered? At times, when we are extremely unhappy with something, we want an instant replacement, or and end to the matter – Pronto! When we see someone wearing (or embracing) something hot and new, we begin to look at what we currently have with less appreciative eyes. Please think about it: Just because you want something so badly, it will NOT be given to you (or will not last very long) when you are FORCING circumstances out of desperation, fear, recklessness, or ego, but instead when you help CREATE circumstances with insight, prudence, patience, effort, & wisdom.

Understand: I'm not proposing you live an ascetic life of constant denial of things that you can afford or are equipped and qualified to receive and appreciate. Not at all! What I am proposing that you learn to be more introspective and ask yourself why you desire the things that you do – fulfillment, necessity, competition, void, pleasure, or vanity. Each of those reasons have corresponding aftereffects that you may or may not want to live with. Each of those reasons will affect your finances, reputation, health and relationships. Each of those reasons reveal your current state of mind, and if you're 'listening' to yourself will indicate if you're primarily behaving with recklessness or discernment – keen insight and judgment.

It's difficult to acquire a disciplined state of mind if you're the sort of woman who always gets her way, who is controlling, who finesses her way out of trouble, or who rarely sees things through.

Today we often hear words tossed around such as perseverance, determination, willpower, fortitude, resilience, or strength as if they are lucky phrases. These words will only have meaning if you meditate on them for deeper meaning. Ponder more frequently on the adage: “Be careful what you wish for because you just might get it”. All too often, it seems that anything we want is ours for the taking.

Many “successful” people will creatively and colorfully boast about their lives that they want you to covet and copy. After you've read or heard their zesty and inspiring words it is up to you to realize that they do not know your circumstances, gifts, weaknesses, history, connections, character, purpose, or obligations. The disciplined mindset means that while it is very important to entertain and act dreams, aspirations and goals in order to live an enriching and fulfilling life however it's important to exercise selectivity, foresight, and to do your due-diligence. It's important to know when to solicit and listen to cheerleaders (people love to jump, cheer and pray when others ask them to) and when to respectfully ask that people not push you onto a path that it's best for you not to get onto.

It's important to pick and choose your pursuits/battles wisely. This means that some things you fight and claw for many not be in your best interests no matter how appealing it may be. Despite your clout, charisma, intellect, or resources, pushing full-steam-ahead in every endeavor, convinced that what you seek is your entitlement, can actually burn you or some bridges out. The disciplined mindset, instead, means that you are shrewdly aware of symptoms that reveal if your vigorous and zealous pursuits will enhance or will complicate your life. What does this mean? In your pursuits: Is what you seek a need or a want? Is your health, finances, relationships, spirituality, or reputation declining in quality? Have you abandoned your values or people that matter the most? Are you ignoring obvious negative consequences? Do you constantly begin and abandon projects due to fleeting distractions or character weakness? Will you be entrapped and enslaved to debilitating habits, schedules, ideas, bills, or people?

Think of self discipline as being the framework of your home – your backbone. Without a solid and strong framework you are like warm gelatin that has no shape or substance, and is subject to being put into anyone's mold which may not be suitable for you at all. Instead, when you have clear definition and a strong awareness of your boundaries, obligations, and purpose they you won't easily break or bend your frame due to every whim or feel or encounter but will be resolute, grounded, and focused.

HOW DOES DISCIPLINING YOURSELF PREVENT YOU FROM

BEING BROKE AND ALONE?

____

____

____

____

____

____

____

____

____

____

____

____

____

____

Love Yourself

"If you aren't good at loving yourself, you'll have a difficult time loving anyone because you'll resent the time and energy you give to another person that you aren't even giving yourself." - Dr. Barbara DeAngelis

LOVE YOURSELF is the greatest power you can have. I did not always love myself because I didn't know how to. I defined love of myself in terms of what I possessed, my career level, what handsome man was on my arm, how much money I had, how popular I was, my zip code, or my waist size. These things I mentioned can (and did) change or be lost. Then what? I no longer deemed myself worthy of love because of what I perceived did not have, and what I allowed to be the 'scale' that I weighed my value upon.

Love for yourself can be seen in: your conversation, presentation, attitude, habits, and relationships. We've heard the scripture, "love your neighbor as yourself". Now, if your relationships are constantly strained, short-lived, or unfulfilled then have you ever considered that it IS you? Why? The way you treat others is very indicative of how you feel about yourself. All the aforementioned chapters are related to this foundation - love of yourself. The magnificent thing about the power of loving yourself is that when it is deeply rooted you are empowered and emboldened from within even in the face of hurt, humiliation, setback, adversity, injustice, tragedy, or attack. That power is not dependent on a lucky charm, mantra, orgasm, paycheck, or red-bottom shoe. That power is not dependent on the weather, size of your nose, length of your hair, number of fans, number of carats owned, or number of organization memberships. That power is dependent on your constant awareness of and fueling your gifts, abilities, and strengths. That power is like that of our sun: It is self sustaining, glowing, burning, unique, and lasting. When that power becomes weakened you're more prone to emitting or attracting negativity, nonsense, narcissism, and neglect. LOVE yourself - Self love can indeed be lost but it can be regained by taking an honest self inventory. There will be some things you do love about yourself and other things that you don't. The absolutely most important thing is to look from your own eyes not your mate's, employer's, parent's, minister's, or friend's. Why? Because their barometer, judgment and their perspective will be through their own eyes and serve as external validation or reinforcement (and that has its own place). Your goal here is to obtain and sustain your own personal, unshakable, and impenetrable self love that deepens on the inside and blossoms outwardly. Once you begin to peel away the negative thoughts, oppressive lies, and other damaging seeds from your inner being then you will see why you are genuinely beautiful and lovable.

Give some thought: Do you know any quality people who are attracted to a person who doesn't love themselves? Do you forgive easily? Are you easily provoked? Are you defensive? Are you controlling? Do you strive to see the good in others? Are you open-minded? Do you neglect, abuse, or berate yourself when you experience heartache or setback? Do you take your own advice that you give to others? Are you hard on others but rationalize your flaws? Do you listen to your body's wellness needs? Your answers to these questions reveal the level of love you have for yourself which will be evident also in how you treat others.

This entire section is meant for you to make sure that you always have deep affection, appreciation, and admiration for yourself. Losing love for yourself is like losing your ability to breathe on your own. Many women are indeed in a vegetative state, living on 'life support', dependent on others to breathe for them. Instead, our love of yourself is your PRIMARY fuel that burns within the very bowels of your being and is not easily extinguished nor is it ever dormant. Your love of yourself is your personal song, your personal romance, your personal creation all of your own design

HOW DOES LOVING YOURSELF PREVENT YOU FROM BEING BROKE AND ALONE?

CONSLUSION

As I've encouraged you throughout this book, you are on a journey that will never be repeated. Your journey can not be walked by anyone else. No one can force you to make adjustments. Please make time for meditative silence and reflection on what you've read and on your notes. Often, many people read books superficially but do not pause and digest necessary points that – when applied – can make their journey less turbulent and more enjoyable.

Change does not happen overnight yet overnight, you can resolve when and how you will begin to improve on being an ever greater woman. I encourage you to open these twelve topics for discussion in your home, circle of girlfriends, to young women, and in your community in order to promote productive dialogue especially regarding topics that diminishes our collective value when we are not our sister's keeper, and watch others fall, and enable each other's crippling habits.

I encourage you to be realistic, balanced and patient with yourself because growing pains can indeed hurt and anyone can relapse. I felt so much warmth and hope for you as I wrote every word from my whole heart as it is my desire for all women to be prized, productive and prosperous. May your beauty, peace, passion, joy, strength and wisdom grow bountifully.

From my heart to yours,

Da-Nel

www.ingramcontent.com/pod-product-compliance
Ingram Content Group UK Ltd.
Pitfield, Milton Keynes, MK11 3LW, UK
UKHW020235250726
13967UKWH00001B/389

9 781257 039357